KITCHEN

Designer

MINI GUIDES
2016

BRIAN RIDER

Kitchen Designer

CHAPTER 1

WHAT IS A DESIGNER

WHAT IS A KITCHEN DESIGNER?

THERE IS A DIFFERENCE BETWEEN PLANNING AND DESIGNING

Anyone new to the industry should concentrate on planning kitchens well and safely. Don't even bother to try and use design concepts unless you and the installer really understand what it is all about.

SAFETY

If you don't plan for safety your are not doing your job.

ERGONOMIC

If you don't allow people & working space the kitchen is useless.

APPLIANCE

Appliances need to be treated with great respect. they cost more than the kitchen.

GET THE BASIC PLANNING RIGHT. THIS IS VASTLY MORE IMPORTANT THAN TRYING TO USE DESIGN THAT THE INSTALLER DOES NOT EVEN UNDERSTAND.

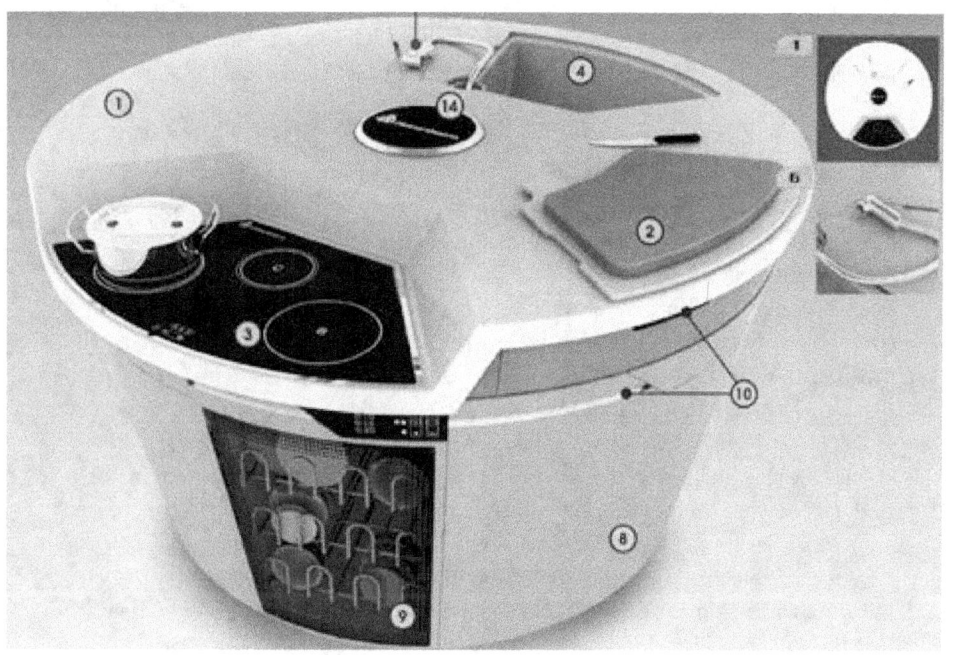

KITCHEN DESIGNER

We have seen literally thousands of kitchen layouts and sadly, many didn't even work let alone be eligible to be Called DESIGNS

FIRSTLY, a kitchen must be able to offer a safe & efficient working environment. Only when it satisfies this condition can it begin to be called a DESIGN. There are many features which lend itself to the term 'DESIGN'. Many of them are quite simple, many are rather complicated and frankly it is best for most KBB planners to stick to plain, simple and efficient plans rather than try to pretend they are capable of creating and executing real kitchen design. We ran a crash course for Wickes personnel some years ago and we suffered the usual abuse from some of the swollen heads in the rank and file but, luckily the head of operations was a canny Scot who had been headhunted from B & Q & knew very well that the majority of his planners did not possess any real knowledge and desperately needed to learn. After a couple of bigheads left the course mid term., they were read the riot act and returned to the course with their tails between their legs. We never had a recurrence of swollen heads to any extent in later courses.

During our time at the RMA, which was easily the top training KBB company at the time we started a series of designer courses. Of the many delegates who attended these specialist courses only 2 delegates really had the knowledge to stay the course and contribute to the finished content. Many of the others went away after 2 or 3 sessions and with some further experience in the field could probably have developed into real designer. None of the big DIY companies were ever able to identify any real potential designers and even a prestigious company such as John Lewis were hard pressed to identify any personnel that could really cut it in the designer stakes.

The problem with a lot of would be designers is that they create various showpieces but really don't know how to execute them or be able to demonstrate to the fitter what their idea really aimed for. During our time with Wickes the showroom design team came up with some really complicated but rather poor design concepts for the showroom. Their head of training at the time was always pleading with them to take on board some really good showroom design ideas that the sales staff could appreciate and their fitters capable of executing. It never happened.

Are there really any hard and fast rules about designing a kitchen? Not really but the ideas must work, must fire the imagination, must be understood by the installer, and must be within the budget the customer is prepared to set.

WHAT HAVE BEEN THE MOST POPULAR DESIGN IDEAS OVER THE YEARS?
In reality the areas that react best to design are the less formal areas of the kitchen such as the eating areas, corner solutions, duplex worktops to use exotic materials efficiently, and the efficient design of peninsula and islands. It is fair to say that the U.S. took to islands very early on and generally use them well but there are some pretty awful examples out there. But islands take up a fair bit of

space if they are to be used efficiently so can you put design into a poky kitchen? The answer is yes but not easy.

The other area where design comes into it's own is lighting and lighting modules. You can design lighting and ventilating modules that not only answer the design aspirations but also become very budget effective. Indeed many of our early kitchen successes were in producing just such examples in the showroom which then caught the buying public's imagination and sold many hundreds of kitchens.

To achieve the end results of selling design we also had to train many fitters in appreciating the concepts of design. We were rewarded with quite a few proud installers taking pictures of their (our) wonderful kitchens and many of them went to work for some of the big names in the industry such as Smallbone and a few went with Smallbone to the U.S.A.

WHAT DO I NEED TO KNOW AS A KITCHEN DESIGNER?

ERGONOMICS AND ANTHROPOMETRICS

KITCHEN ZONES

DOUBLE WORK TRIANGLE

ISLANDS AND PENINSULA

EATING ZONES

30° AND 45ª SOLUTIONS

PRESENTATION TECHNIQUES

PERSONAL VS SALEABLE

CATERING VS DOMESTIC

KITCHEN STORAGE

IN THE ROUND

Clean crisp and frankly boring. it is simply a collection of design ideas but no intelligent execution. In a room of this size I would have expected a more efficient kitchen not just a pretty kitchen.

Clearly we do not know the customer spec but I would estimate that the price charged did not leave a delighted customer

Masterpiece

This takes the classic German concept of a tall wall, which was first used in the 1950's and translates it to a modern masterpiece. But in reality you have a very inefficient kitchen. Loads of storage space but hardly any worktop space.

Unfortunately the planner in this instance seems to have forgotten the basic kitchen concepts of the working triangle and working space for appliances.

LARGE COUNTRY KITCHEN

Kitchen a la Smallbone & two of everything. But this should be considered as a kitchen with two chefs and should incorporate a double working triangle. It does not work. Nor does there appear to be any efficient ventilation and the kitchen is woefully short of worktop especially in the cooking and preparation areas.

IN THE ROUND

    This has been a feature of Italian kitchens for many years and the aspiration of British Kitchen manufacturers and suppliers for decades. It is a lovely theme but very expensive and it is still necessary to apply the working rules properly. Do you think these domino hobs have been dealt with safely?

Island Moden

---- 4 ----

ISLANDS

Islands and peninsula must answer the 900, 750, 1200 and 1000 rules. It is almost certain that they will need to conform to the 2-chef triangle.

Check out these islands and decide what your critique is then compare with our critique at the end of this subject.

Island Table

Island Microwave

Island Blonde

rustic island with peninsula

ISLAND DESIGNING

1) Make sure you follow all the dimensional space rule.

2) Do not place a working zone on the island that is directly opposite another working zone. i.e. a hob directly opposite a sink.

3) where space permits design a double work triangle - providing it's own sink and hob and even fridge, if possible.

4) A double work triangle can include just a microwave but if possible an oven would be useful or perhaps an oven microwave at a pinch.

5) don't forget the gadget space. the sous chef will almost certainly be using some kitchen gadgets such as mixers of blender.

6) the spatial requirements of an island would be 1000mm separation from a working zone to the perimeter worktop or 900mm where no working zone exists. Remember these are minimum allowances not optimum. As with anywhere in the kitchen always allow 1200mm if available. Also remember your eating area requirements. Minimum eating place area is 500 x 350 and ideally you should always strive for 600 width or greater.

ISLAND CRITIQUE

ISLAND CRITIQUE

Island Modern
The best layout so far but not enough worktop & the place setting on the left hand stool is inadequate.

Island Microwave
Typical U.S. kitchen with a U.S. range. But why right up against a wall? Not even tiled? Why the microwave in the island? When you get older you don't want to keep bending down to look in the window. the island is not greatly productive but better than many.

Island Table
It reminds me of Judy Steele's Scottish tower house kitchen. We offered to design her kitchen for free and get some magazine coverage but she wasn't really interested in design and just wanted a dirty great table in the centre of the room, dominating the room as she was used to. Ridiculous.

Island Blonde

This looks more the business even got a computer niche but frankly the worktop space is inadequate and does not begin to offer a double work triangle. The tall wall is a bit of a disaster, as it usually is, with totally inadequate set down space. But it is pretty. I find stools very uncomfortable but they look better in the picture.

Island Rustic

A great attempt to produce a cotttagey kitchen and lots of chairs. But they are a bit ugly. This is effectively a peninsula kitchen with an island but as most of the worktop space is set aside for eating the actual working space is somewhat restricted and the tall cluster in the corner ensures that the double working triangle even in this large kitchen, does not exist. But again it is pretty.

CONCLUSION.

Having studied 100's of islands I have to say that most of them don't really work but if you took some of these ideas and put them together you could come up with a working solution that people could use and enjoy and even sell to other people.

REMEMBER - A kitchen is a failure if it does not appeal to more than one person.

THE ISSUE/QUESTION OF DESIGN

70% of buyers don't need or want design but that still leaves 30%???

would you really pay £1000's for this piece of cramped design?

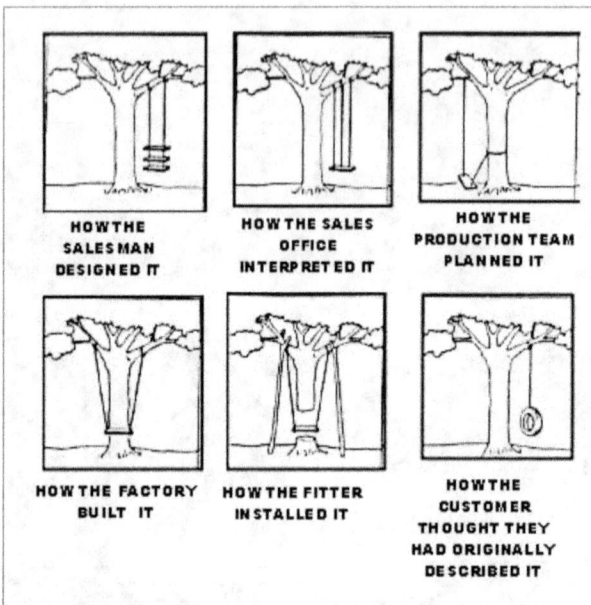

HOW THE SALESMAN DESIGNED IT

HOW THE SALES OFFICE INTERPRETED IT

HOW THE PRODUCTION TEAM PLANNED IT

HOW THE FACTORY BUILT IT

HOW THE FITTER INSTALLED IT

HOW THE CUSTOMER THOUGHT THEY HAD ORIGINALLY DESCRIBED IT

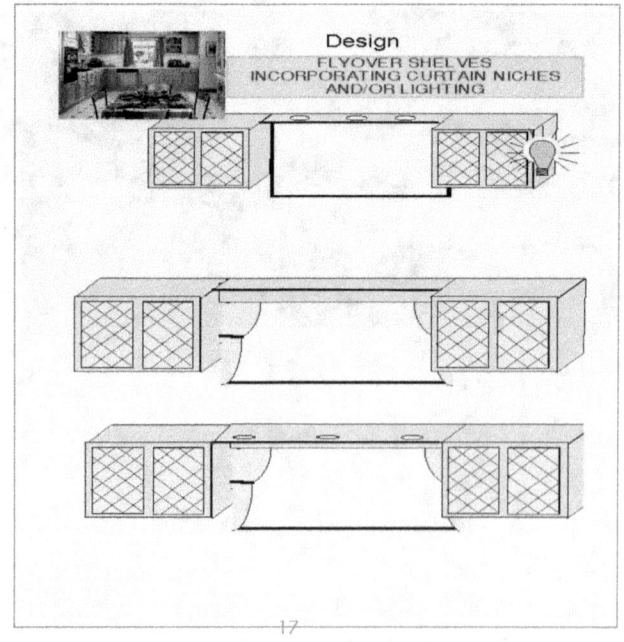

Design

FLYOVER SHELVES INCORPORATING CURTAIN NICHES AND/OR LIGHTING

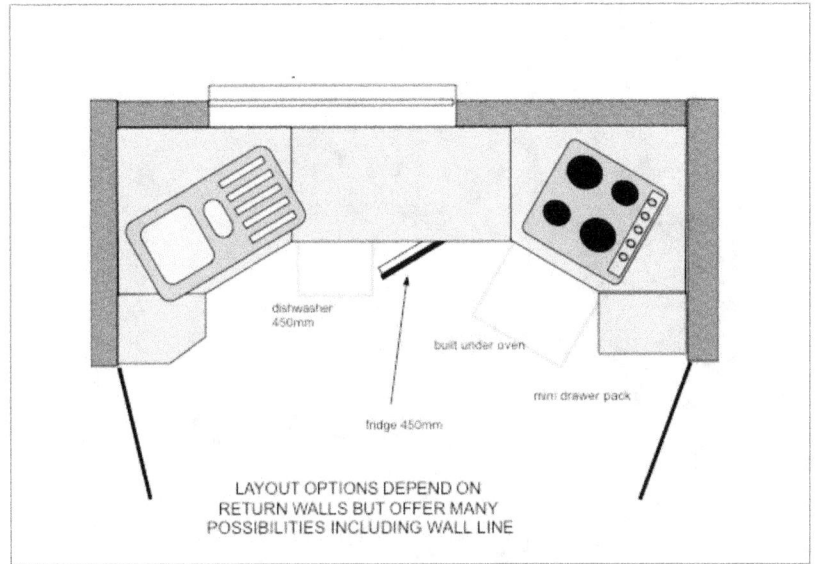

dishwasher 450mm

built under oven

mini drawer pack

fridge 450mm

LAYOUT OPTIONS DEPEND ON
RETURN WALLS BUT OFFER MANY
POSSIBILITIES INCLUDING WALL LINE

Although planners and designers are used to 45° solutions very few attempt the more advanced and more versatile 30° solutions. You may know that the 45° triangle has the relationship of 1 - and the square root of 2. You probably don`t know that the 30° triangle has the relationship of 1 - 2 and the square root of 3. Hinge manufacturers all produce 45° hinges and many produce 30° hinges so you can design cabinets to suit both arrangements and some manufacturers provide ready made units: See the new dedicated section.

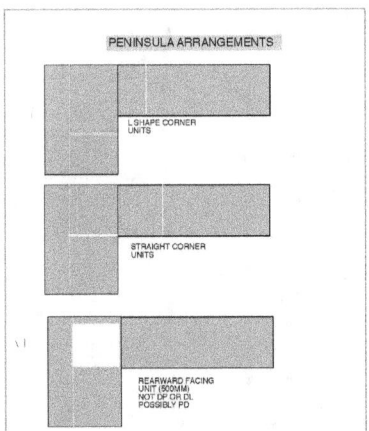

PENINSULA ARRANGEMENTS

L SHAPE CORNER
UNITS

STRAIGHT CORNER
UNITS

REARWARD FACING
UNIT (500MM)
NOT DF OR DL
POSSIBLY PD

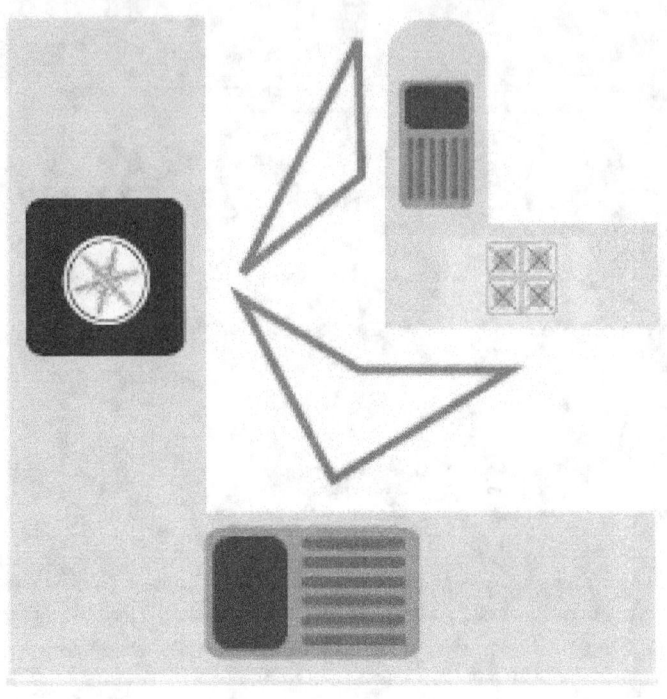

TWO CHEF KITCHEN

DOUBLE WORKING TRIANGLE

To make this sort of kitchen work with two chefs it must be of a quite considerable size and almost certainly will require an Island.

We will usually expect one chef to be the main chef and the other is the sous chef. the main chef will have the main triangle centred around a large sink and dishwasher, large fridge and full cooking area. The sous chef will usually share the large fridge but will have his/her own hob area - possibly specialised and almost certainly a 2 burner induction. And will usually have a smaller sink on the island which can be used for prep and cleaning.

The sous chef will usually be delegated about 1 metre of worktop space as a minimum and probably will have only one or two small gadgets. The sous chef will probably work in a 2.5 m triangle.

When we first introduced the concept of a double working triangle back in the 1980's a lot of delegates scoffed at the idea. However, today, as we know, many families have two chefs working in the same kitchen and not just as an alternative. When creating a large family meal for guests this can involve a number of dishes and some of these will be specialist dishes that Dad or one of the kids may be trying to perfect. they will want to be in complete control of their area of the kitchen and the appliances they need.

It is also very important that the sous chef does not get in the way of the main chef and can carry our his/her tasks with complete independence but still co-ordinated for the final result.

It is also quite probable that the sous chef will be working on solus meals but will want to use their own dishes and appliances.

They say that kitchens are now 30% smaller than the 60"s but they have not considered some of these big country homes and barn conversions where the kitchens are quite enormous and can easily accommodate this kind of concept.

This sort of kitchen will almost certainly incorporate a large ice n water fridge or possibly even a his and hers fridge. Our last kitchen had just such a twin two door Liebherr fridge arrangement

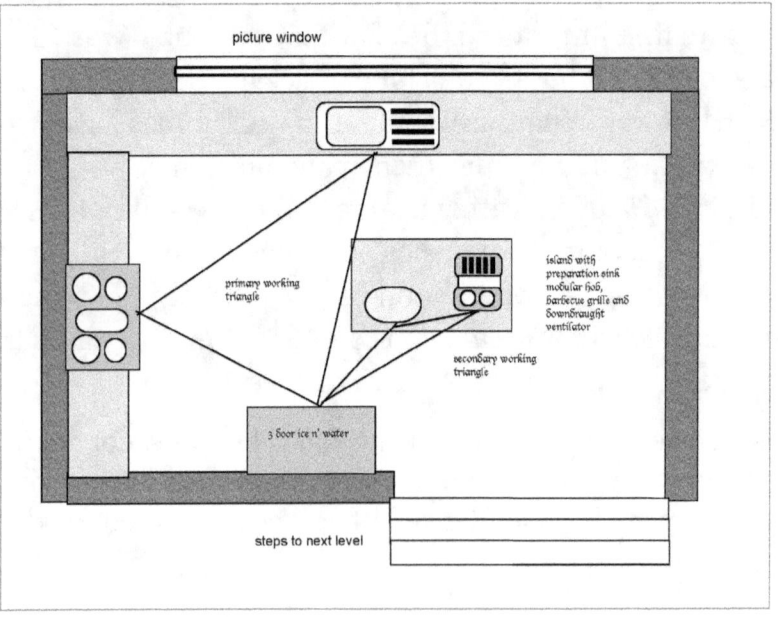

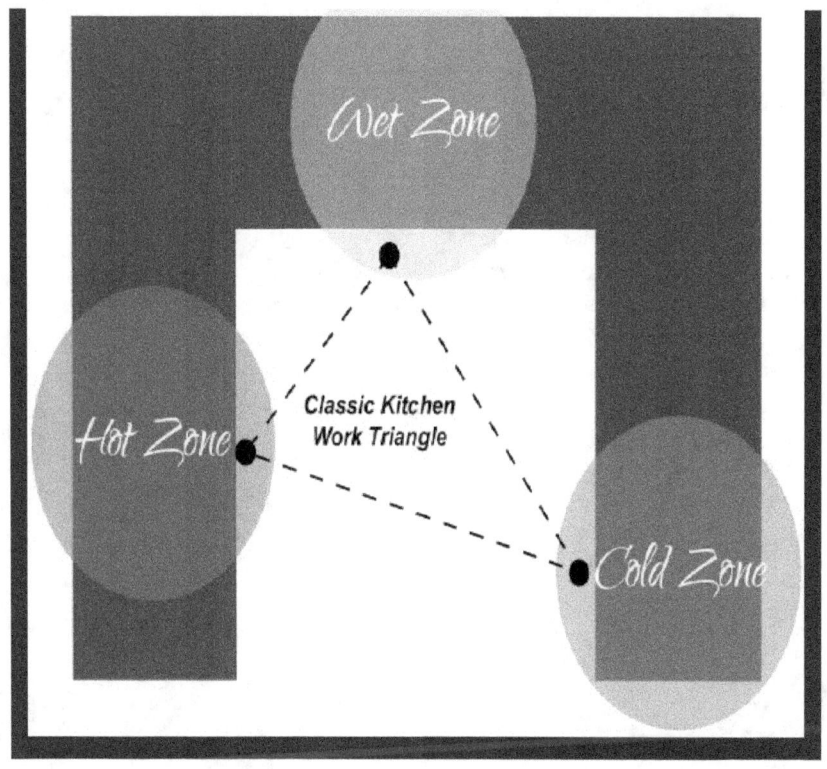

CREATING THE ZONES

The kitchen zones can come in a variety of guises and many zones may be created by the Chef or the Sous Chef. For example the Sous chef might favour a microwave oven for his/her main work and an Induction hob for hob top cooking. Clearly the preparation zone should be near these two facilities. For example the Sous Chef might also favour a multi function Food Mixer for his/her main dishes. As these tend to be quite large items and often with a considerable amount of accessories you may need to set aside quite a bit of storage in addition to worktop space. With the availability of 45cm dishwashers there is now clearly a case for providing the sous chef with his/her own dishwasher station. I am sure many of you will already have found how difficult it is for two chefs to share the same dishwashers, especially with large mixing bowls.

Similarly with an induction hob there are many pans that cannot be used and will require separate storage and easy access to the sous chef. The sous chef might also evolve a requirement for certain cooking dishes for the microwave station. Two chefs can easily get on each other's nerves

Not everyone will require the same zones and double chef kitchens will need extra zones such as baking

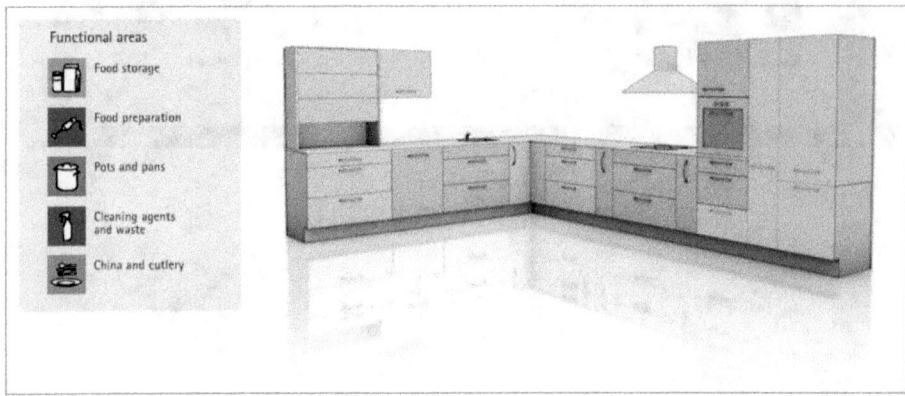

4 i8 1: TV, CD, DVD und Radio

MEDIA CENTRE

The media centre concept for the kitchen has gone way beyond the little TV in the corner perhaps with a built in dvd. Even the more sophisticated 4 in one flip down sets do not inspire the more modern households.

People are now getting used to bigger and bigger tv and bigger and better pictures. These larger screens have also come into the monitor market so it is possible to link a computer to an HD ready large screen 32" monitor or bigger. If you have got an 85" giant viewscreen in the living room it is unlikely you will be satisfied with a 10" flip down when you go into the kitchen.

As they have now twinned these entertainment centres to high quality and yet compact sound systems the whole market is open either for the ambitious product supplier or more probably a high quality bespoke kitchen designer with some quality fabricating equipment and/or skilful installers. With the modern solid surface materials there is no reason why an imaginative designer could not come up with something not only elegant but eminently usable as well. What better than to sit in the kitchen while the food is being prepared and doing your days work at the same time.

There are increasingly a wide range of media products that can be used in the kitchen but now is the time to make the widest possible interpretation of the products and usage.

In larger households and particularly an American household a great deal of time is spent in the kitchen which may even have a family room attached.

It is clear therefore that an entertainment centre is probably not only attractive but essential. And what about the toddlers? They will also need entertainment while mum does the chores (or maybe even a house dad?)

Clearly a computer will have an air of necessity in a busy kitchen such as this. The cook of the house will certainly want to access his/her recipes on the computer and perhaps even cook along with their favourite food show?

There certainly are a plethora of choices with the various wifi facilities available using an all in one computer such as an Apple with a built in or wall hung option of a computer of whatever sort and a monitor perhaps interlinking with a tablet. The options are virtually limitless and the range of costs similarly. It just takes a little understanding on the planners part.

This is not only a three door ice 'n water fridge it also provides TV, DVD, CD and has a host of computer functions. - I want one!

The image below is a fully fledged media centre and can have a fully functioning computer such as an Apple 27" cinema screen and using a wireless keyboard you can sit at the breakfast bar and enjoy a whole media experience.

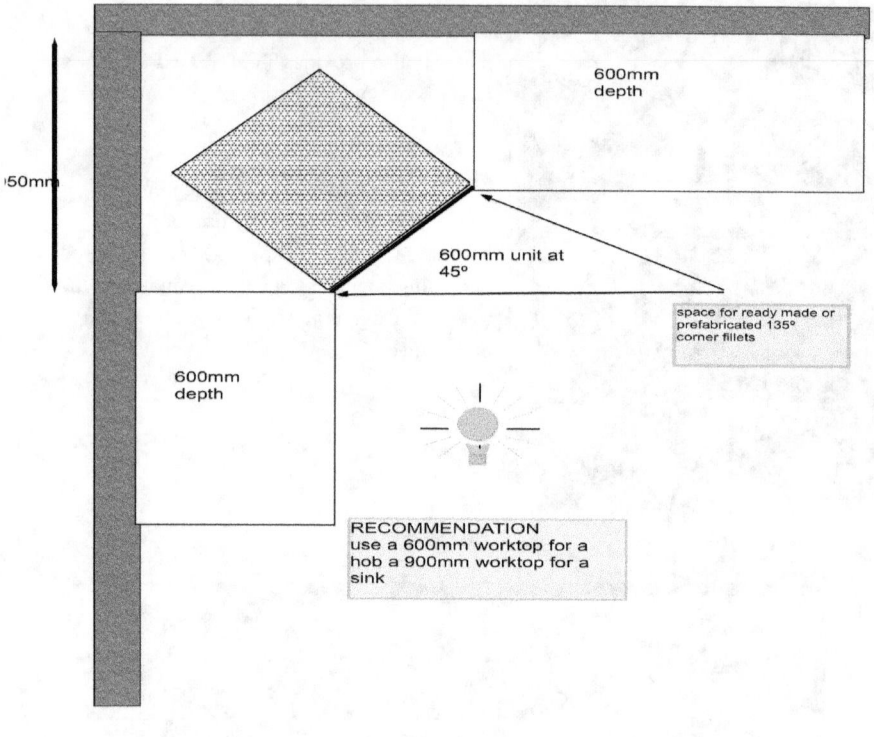

600mm
depth

50mm

600mm unit at
45°

space for ready made or
prefabricated 135°
corner fillets

600mm
depth

RECOMMENDATION
use a 600mm worktop for a
hob a 900mm worktop for a
sink

9

45° AND 30° CORNER SOLUTIONS

Most kitchen ranges now include a standard 45° solution with prefabricated corner posts but some ranges also include units made at 45° but not always with corner posts The corner post is essential to avoid clashing of drawers and doors but any kitchen fitter with even a modicum of experience would be aware of the need for fitting corner posts even if they are not supplied. Clearly you need to calculate for the setting out dimension including the corner posts.

The corner post is essential to avoid clashing of drawers and doors but any kitchen fitter with even a modicum of experience would be aware of the need for fitting corner posts even if they are not supplied. Clearly you need to calculate for the setting out dimension including the corner posts.

A standard setting out dimension is 1050 x 1050. We know that the relationship of a 45° triangle is as per the diagram i.e. 1:1 and the square root of 2. If we take a standard 60 cm unit and turn it to 45° we can calculate the setting out dimension.

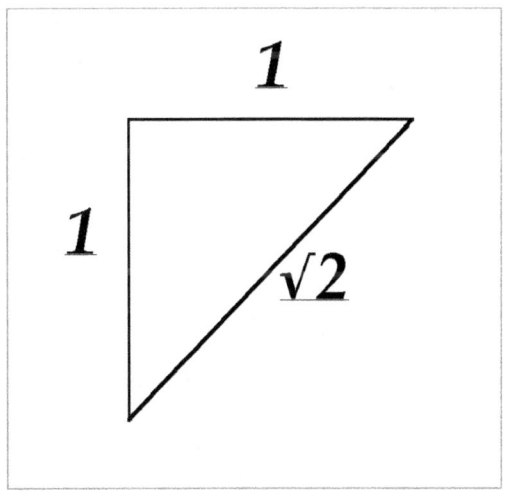

So starting with the assumption that the unit is 600mm with a 600 door we can now transpose our key dimensions into our example triangle or unit

If you calculate the value of the sqaure root of 2 this translates into a number of 1,414???

We than multiply our unit measurement of 600 by this square root and you then calculate the measurement on the next diagram

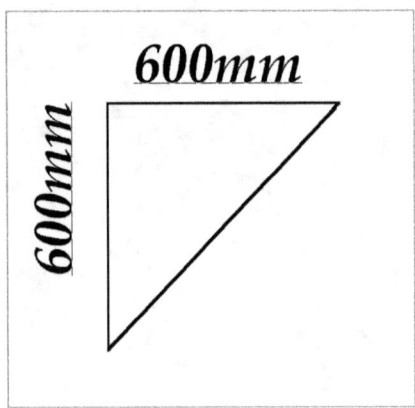
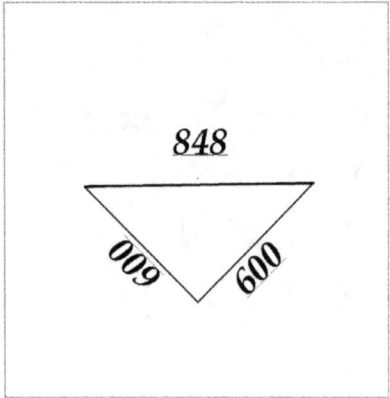

But this is just one component of the setting out dimension so we need to calculate the space occupied by the carcase when turned to 45°

As you can see using the reverse calculation we can see this measurement is 424mm this is also 50% of the total carcase setting out dimension which comes as no surprise as this is an isosceles triangle. So now we need to calculate the dimensions of the 45° often refered to as 135° corner posts (90+45)

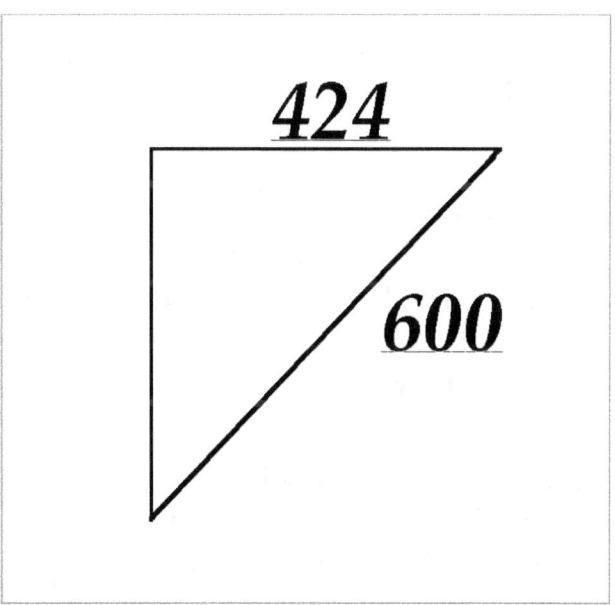

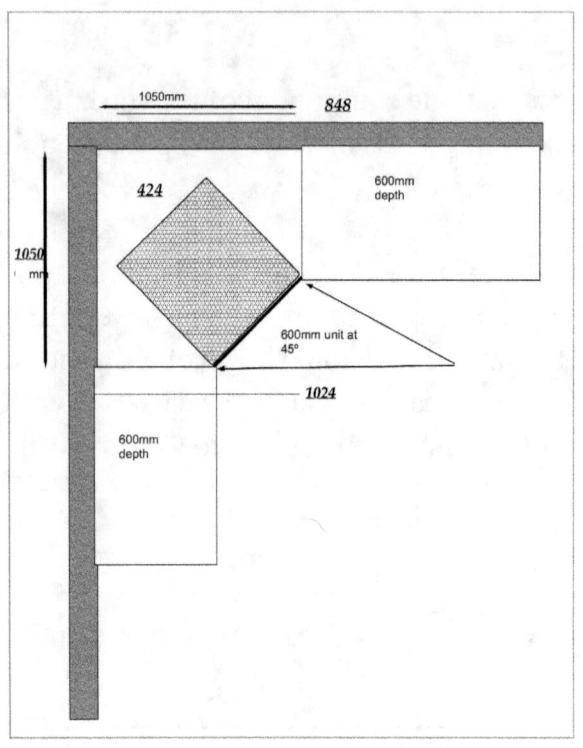

So to the final argument;- we have shown that the carcase occupies a space of 848mm when turned to 45°. But the carcase has to be pulled out to 600mm to match up with the worktop but it only occupies a space of 424mm on this part of the worktop so we have the difference of 176mm to add to our setting out dimension. Adding these two components gives us a grand total of 1024 which actually equates to some of the manufacturer`s setting out dimensions as specified in their catalogues. How can this be? We know we need corner posts otherwise the doors foul.

But what we haven`t calculated is the actually carcase dimension rather than the normal dimension.

A carcase is around 570mm or even less without the door. The door will add 15 - 20 mm but this is not quite as wide as the carcase and more often than not has rounded edges so this would leave around 20mm for the corner posts or possibly just a thickness of carcase material around 15-19 mm - adequate but not always safe. this resulted in most manufacturers adopting the 1050 setting out for a more substantial corner post and greater safety.

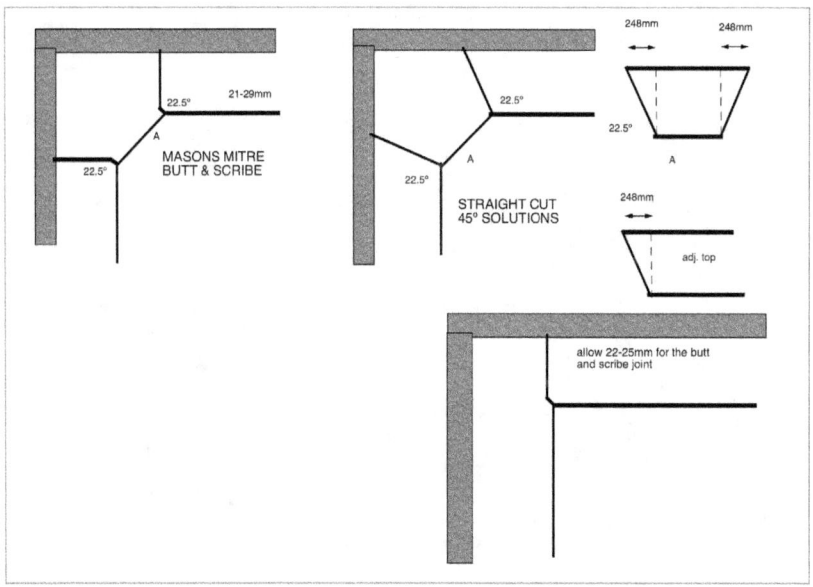

ALTERNATIVE 45°
SOLUTIONS

UNIT SIZE	SETTING OUT DIMENSION		WORKTOP SIZE
600	1050 X 1050		636
500		979	536
400		908	436
300		837	336

THESE ARE THE POPULAR
STANDARD SIZE SOLUTIONS BUT
CAN BE ARRANGED FOR ANY
BASE SETTING
SUCH AS 1024 X 1024
OR 1088 BY 1088
USING THE 71 MM ADJUSTMENT
ALONG THE SETTING OUT
DIMENSION FOR EVERY 100 MM
ALONG THE FRONT.

100	71	

45° CORNER SOLUTIONS

THE OLD METHOD - BUILD A WALL

MASSIVE LOSS OF VISUAL AND ACTUAL SPACE

45° CORNER SOLUTIONS

THE OLD METHOD - BUILD A WALL

MASSIVE LOSS OF VISUAL AND ACTUAL SPACE

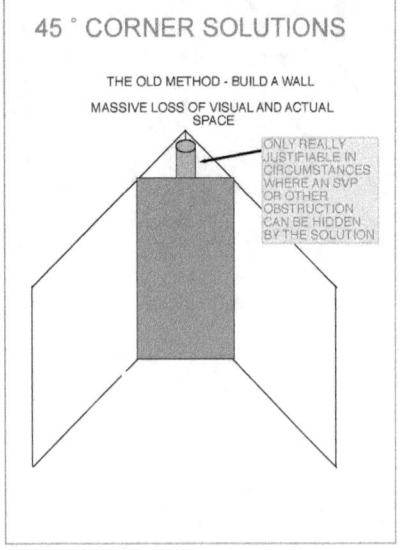

ONLY REALLY
JUSTIFIABLE IN
CIRCUMSTANCES
WHERE AN SVP
OR OTHER
OBSTRUCTION
CAN BE HIDDEN
BY THE SOLUTION

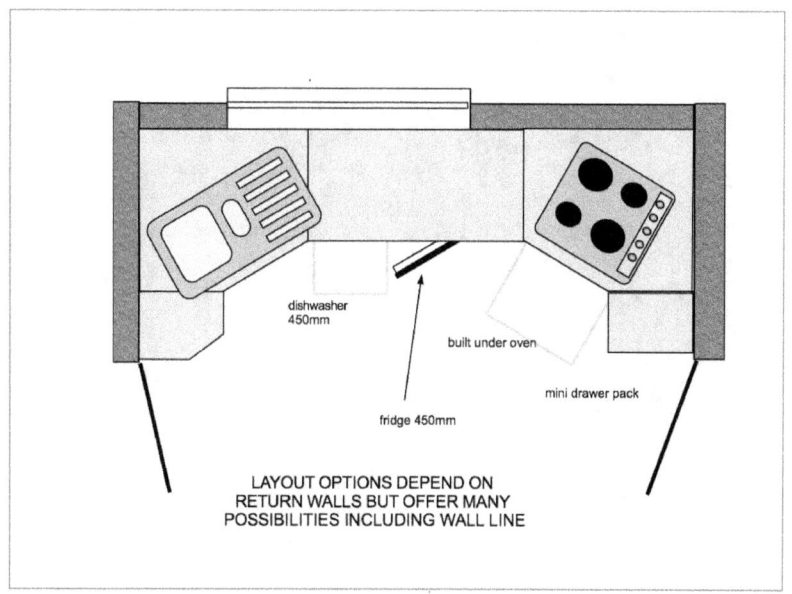

dishwasher
450mm

built under oven

mini drawer pack

fridge 450mm

LAYOUT OPTIONS DEPEND ON
RETURN WALLS BUT OFFER MANY
POSSIBILITIES INCLUDING WALL LINE

10

30° SOLUTIONS

We started to use 30° solutions in the 80's and produced comprehensive setting out sheets but most of the delegates weren't really quite at that level yet so the method didn't develop very quickly. Both German & Italian hinge manufacturers produced the special cranked hinges for both 45° and 30° units but few manufacturers were brave enough to use them despite their obvious advantages. I remember visiting a Tiles r Us store where we did a lot of training and development and was asked by a kitchen designer of many years experience "has anyone worked out what angle these units are? My fitters have problems with mitring the mouldings?" I was a little shocked & disappointed by the level of non comprehension and didn't have the heart to point out the obvious. To this day I don't know whether he ever bothered to find out. This designer also attended one of our advanced level design courses and it was obvious he didn't have any desire to learn and frankly didn't want to learn. I would urge the readers to try these solutions, they are not only stylish they are extremely practical, especially with hi tech worktops.

So let us calculate the value of ?. As we can see the relationship of a 30° triangle is 1, 2 and the square root of 3. The value of $\sqrt{3}$ which you can easily find on your calculator is 1.732 so if we use a 300mm door which provides a 150mm projection and then multiply this value by $\sqrt{3}$ we get the value of $\doteq$ 260mm. Which basically means that a unit with a 300mm door set to 30° will occupy a space of 260mm plus any spacing you may provide.

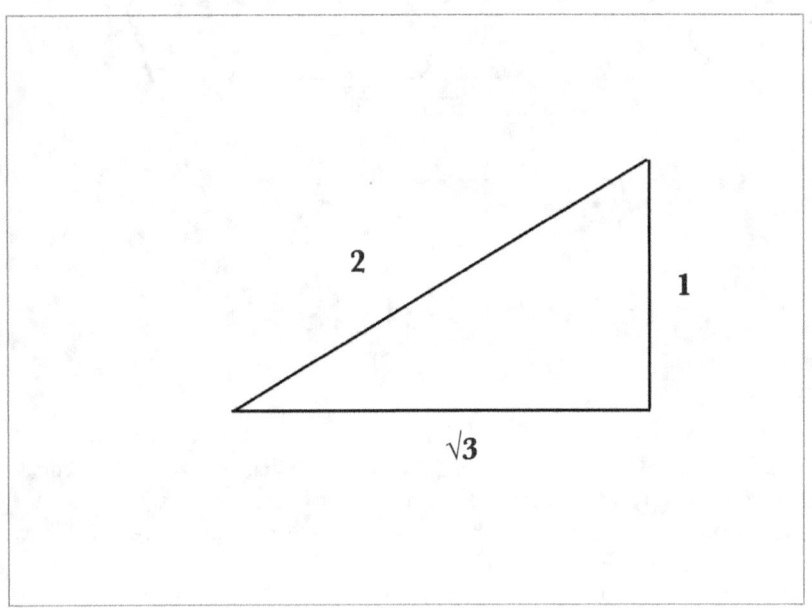

Clearly if you are using an open shelf like a wine rack no spacing is required. Or if you use a door, just a carcase filler of 15mm or 18mm can be used. For appliances with large doors you may need to use a larger filler such as a light pelmet moulding or worktop edging or w.h.y. [what have you]. So our example kitchen including fillers would occupy a space of around 3.2m but by reducing the depth of the units at either end you could reduce this to around 3m.

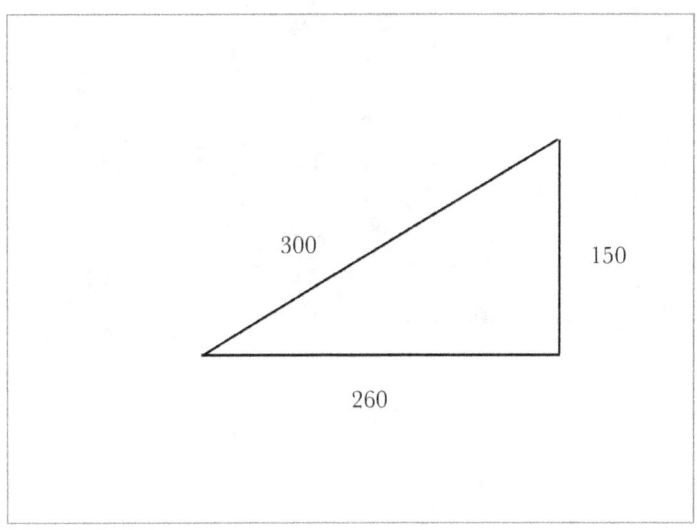

THE MEZZANINE SOLUTION

A linear corner is not workable either psychologically or practically. The ergonomics of a corner are quite simply unworkable for the normal homo sapien. You feel uncomfortable unless you are working against flat worktop. Try standing at the V of the corner - it feels unnaturally weird and uncomfortable. The L shape sinks have the same problem . They are just not natural. The hob in this illustration not only looks ridiculous it has been cut right over a worktop joint - not a clever thing to do.

The German kitchen planners and installers very early decided that a 45° solution is the best for a working corner and set down the sizes necessary to accommodate a standard solution with corner posts to ensure doors do not clash. Unfortunately they didn't take it far enough and most solutions involved cutting off the corner with a false wall - what a waste you could bury your grandmother there.

I hope you can see in these various examples that the 45° corners are much more attractive and actually release the corner space to be a real working space. But wasting all that room?? There are occasionally excuses for doing this possibly because there is a chimney in the corner or a large flu. But for no reason? The other problem with the 45 corner is the worktop. Early worktops were only available in set sizes so to find a top to fit the entire corner is difficult and expensive. At best you might just manage it out of a Duropal 1000mm double round and in most cases you would have to source a 1200 double round to do the job efficiently. Very expensive

2 corners of the same kitchen - the 45 corner looks great but they have cut off a great chunk of the room - frankly amateurish

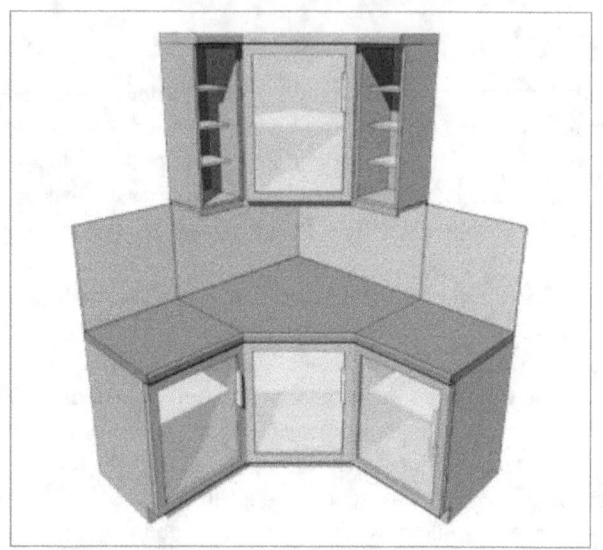

very attractive but the worktops would cost a fortune

Very early we realized that using big expensive tops to create a corner solution was wasteful - even in a showroom.

The idea of the mezzanine shelf started to germinate early on but it was when we were funding our own showrooms - mostly on a shoestring - we realized there must be a better way and so the mezzanine shelf or top was born.

Quite simply the idea was to use only standard 600mm worktops which are readily and cheaply available. That means the mezzanine shelf is a separate small piece placed usually around plinth height at the rear of the corner solution. You can even use the sink cut out on many occasions with a separate edging material such as wood edge.

The result is very attractive but also more welcoming than the expensive oversize top. As the mezzanine is higher than the surround worktops anything placed on it is more accessible, even behind a hob.

This solution can be executed in all worktop materials and is a real money saver and yet is a much more exciting solution than the alternatives. Just have a look at some of these various worktop solutions including tiled areas.

We have taught this solution over many years but I have to say that with the DIY stores we used to have a lot of apathy towards even such an obvious benefit. Strangely we had much more success with the Dutch and the mezzanine solution appeared very early in many kitchens planned in the Netherlands. We have also used the same method to create linear worktop extensions and have used this in conjunction with duplex tops to avoid complicated jointing. In a corner you can use different heights for the corner than the adjacent tops and therefore only butt joints.

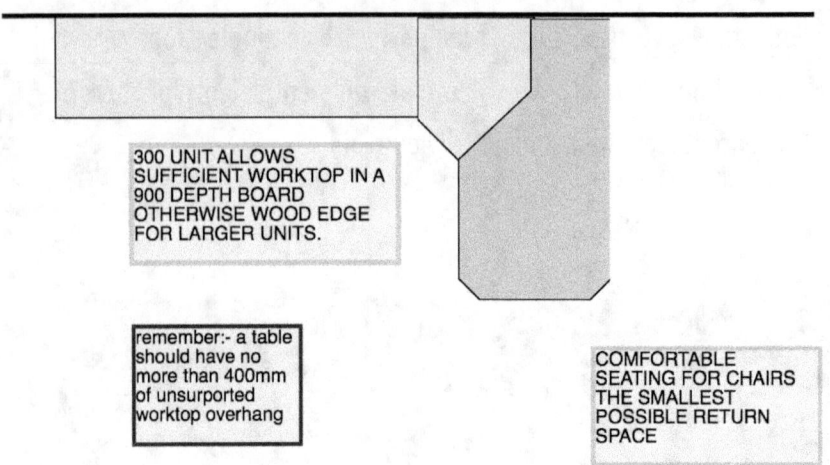

300 UNIT ALLOWS
SUFFICIENT WORKTOP IN A
900 DEPTH BOARD
OTHERWISE WOOD EDGE
FOR LARGER UNITS.

remember:- a table
should have no
more than 400mm
of unsurported
worktop overhang

COMFORTABLE
SEATING FOR CHAIRS
THE SMALLEST
POSSIBLE RETURN
SPACE

12

EATING AREAS

We found many years ago that eating areas had a very great appeal in the kitchen and made a project easily saleable so we would try to incorporate one in every design if at all possible. A lot of the ideas are easily attainable with modest materials

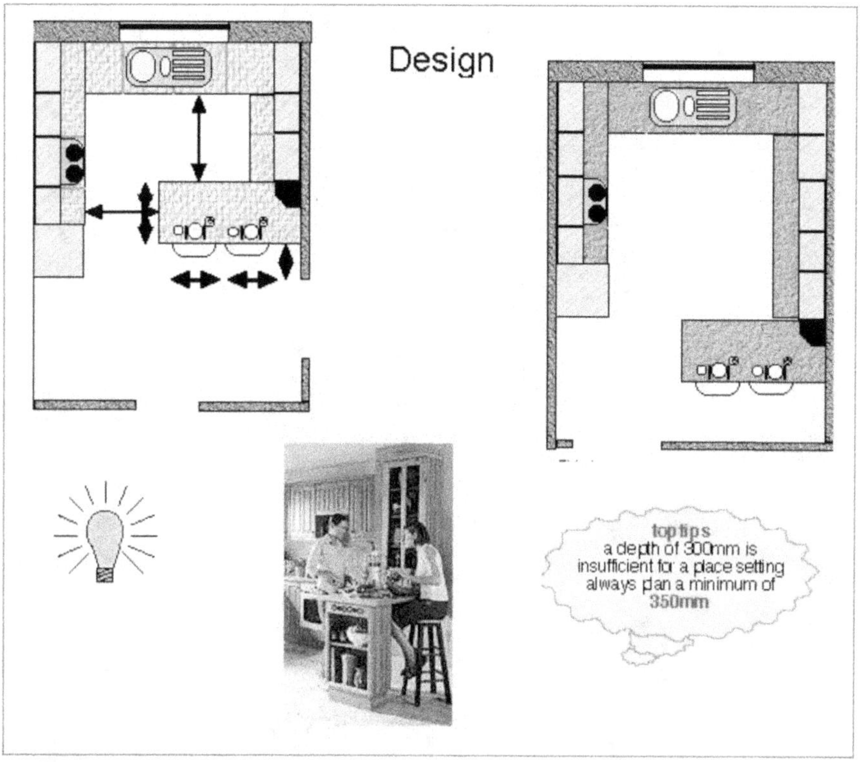

Design

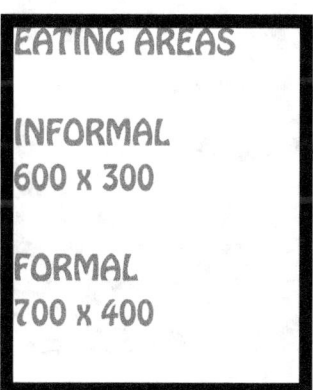

EATING AREAS

INFORMAL
600 x 300

FORMAL
700 x 400

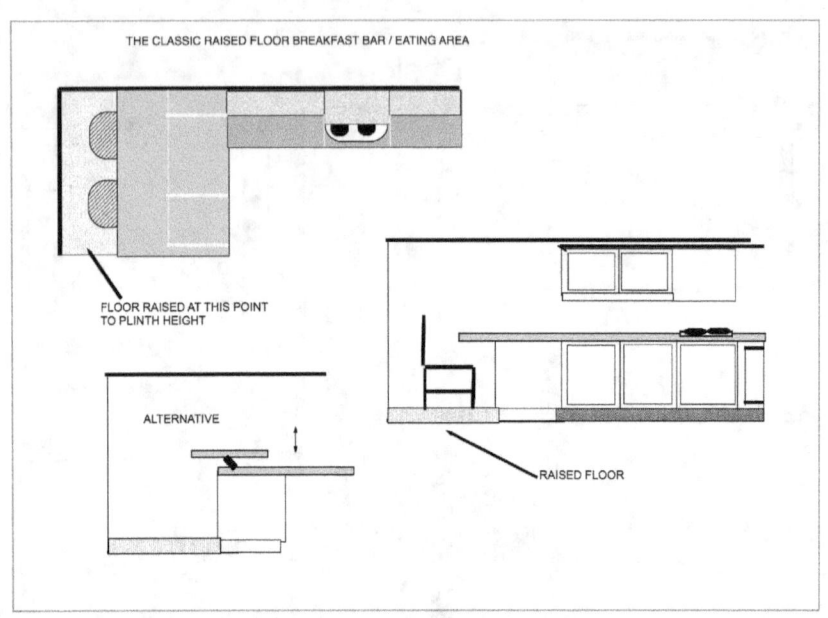

THE CLASSIC RAISED FLOOR BREAKFAST BAR / EATING AREA

FLOOR RAISED AT THIS POINT TO PLINTH HEIGHT

ALTERNATIVE

RAISED FLOOR

13

STORAGE

Although we have covered basic storage under the unit construction section in the kitchen planning guide, advanced srorage is is an important subject so I thought we should emphasise some of the key points. In particular check out Hafele, Kessebohmer and the emerging players in the market

DESIGN - BESPOKE

14

This section requires a real dedicated designer who has the ability to visualize a design study but even more importantly must be able to execute the project. It is pointless designing a dream that no one can create. Design can be traditional or modern.

The definition of design is tenuous but essentially it is using your product in a more imaginative and innovative way & adding to or modifying the basic units to provide a more attractive &efficient end user experience.

What design isn't! is to offer arty farty creations that don't work but may look ok. If we study the kitchen below we can evaluate. This kitchen works on an aesthetic level but as a practical working kitchen it is a joke. The tall wall is simply unworkable and the fridge would struggle to keep it's temperature. There is very little usable worktop space for the ovens or the fridge. For such an expensive kitchen there appears to be no preparation area except the island & its circular bowl. But the bowl in a not in a convenient position . But it is very pretty and with some rethinking on the tall wall it would make both a stunning looking kitchen and a quality working kitchen. Can't see a lot of lighting either

OVEN HOB FRIDGE QUESTION

DON`T PLACE AN OVEN & FRIGE SIDE BY SIDE LEAVE AT LEAST 300MM BETWEEN THE TWO

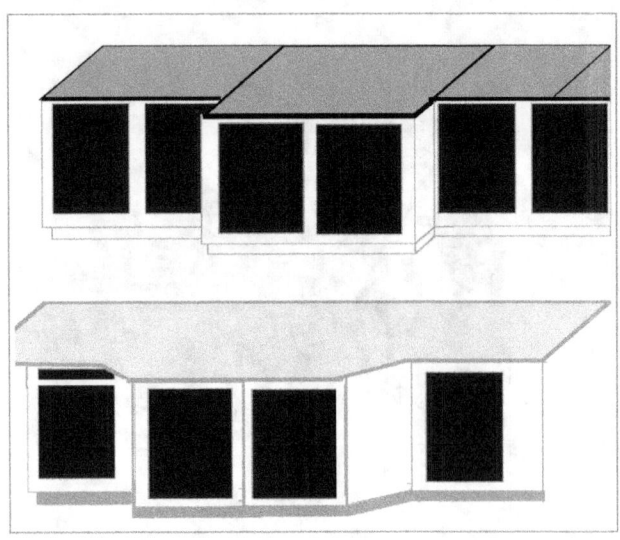

3d units are expensive but you can use a 3d worktop for similar effect

Thank you for purchasing this latest version of our 2016 mini guides. The Kitchen Designer guide is the first of the designer guides which have only been touched on in previous full sized guides. For the first time you have enough material to progress fully into an AKBB PROF Designer qualification.

We want you to enjoy this publication and learn from it,

To this end we offer TOTAL SUPPORT - if you feel you need help or clarification on any points please log in to our website at

www.kbb2000.com

KITCHEN PLANNING ESSENTIALS	**I POINT PERSPECTIVE & VANISHING POINT**
KITCHEN PLANNING APPLIANCES ESSENTIALS	**2 POINT PERSPECTIVE & VANISHING POINT**
KITCHEN DESIGN	**BIRDS EYE PERSPECTIVE**
BATHROOM PLANNING	**BEDROOM PRESENTATION**
BATHROOM DESIGN	**BATHROOM PRESENTATION**

SURVEYING
TECHNIQUES

EXTERIOR
PRESENTATIONS

GRANNY
FLATS

CLOAK ROOMS
DRESSING ROOMS
CLOSETS

KITCHEN
WORKING
TRIANGLE 3:1:6

*DOUBLE
WORKING
TRIANGLE*

CREATIVE
INTERIOR DESIGN
USING A
COMPUTER

CAD VS BRAIN

www.ingramcontent.com/pod-product-compliance
Lightning Source LLC
Chambersburg PA
CBHW071253280526
45788CB00004B/1709